LONDON

Designed and Produced by

Ted Smart & David Gibbon

MAYFLOWER BOOKS, INC.,
NEW YORK 10022.

Introduction

"When a man is tired of London, he is tired of life, for there is in London all that life can afford."

These famous words of Dr Johnson are as true today as when he uttered them 200 years ago. London can claim as much, if not more, variety of atmosphere, culture, entertainment, tradition and architecture as any city on earth.

Packed into the 610 square miles of Greater London – Europe's largest city – are a wealth of concert halls, art galleries, museums, parks and gardens, theatres, cinemas, restaurants and famous buildings which in recent years have drawn increasing numbers of tourists from Europe, the Far East and particularly the United States. More than ten million people now visit Britain each year and nearly all of them will spend part of their holiday in the capital.

With its "bobbies", its red double-decker buses and its famous underground system among its most instantly identifiable features, London has an unhurried air of permanence reinforced by the durability of its great institutions such as the Tower, St Pauls, Buckingham Palace and Big Ben.

There is much more to London than visits to these famous tourist spots. The traveller who forsakes the guided tours for a day or two and wanders at will will come across some of the winding streets and narrow alleys so reminiscent of the city Dickens knew. One of the pleasures of London is that so much can be seen on foot – safely and without needing to walk more than two or three miles a day.

Starting perhaps from Piccadilly Circus – once regarded as the hub of the old British Empire – head south down Lower Regent Street into St James's which has remained largely unchanged for three centuries. Continue down St James's Street to St James's Palace, built by Henry VIII as a royal residence, until Queen Victoria foresook it for Buckingham Palace at the start of her reign. But its links with the British Royal Family remain, albeit tenuously. When a new foreign ambassador arrives to take up residence in London he establishes his right to do so by presenting his credentials "at the Court of St James".

St James's also houses two of London's leading clubs for gentlemen – the Reform in Pall Mall where Jules Verne's Phileas Fogg set off to travel Around the World in Eighty Days, and the distinguished Athenaeum whose members include many Lords, Knights, Government ministers and leading figures of the arts, sciences and public life. Close by, in St James's Street itself, are two delightful old shops which have been catering to the needs of such club members for more than a century: Lobbs, whose tailor-made shoes adorn the feet of royalty and the famous, and Lock's who have been making hats for more than two hundred years.

A ten-minute walk across St James's Park leads into Whitehall where the solid facades of Government buildings look on to quiet quadrangles and discreet side streets. Even Downing Street, where the Prime Minister resides at Number Ten, has an air on an early Sunday morning of a respectable little residential street. Only the ever-present policeman at the door suggests something more significant.

Up Whitehall, into Trafalgar Square to feed the perpetually hungry pigeons and to admire the 200-foot-high Nelson's Column and Landseer's Lions, then up into St Martin's Lane where every other building seems to be a pub or a theatre. On both sides of this attractive street are a host of little courts and alleys, well stocked with specialist and antiquarian bookshops and antique dealers. In Goodwin's Court, off to the right, there are some delightful Georgian houses now occupied exclusively by people or companies connected with the arts – writers, publishers, film companies and so on.

Continue up St Martin's Lane, through Cambridge Circus and into Charing Cross Road, the centre of London's book trade, then turn left into the narrow streets of world-famous Soho.

Soho was developed after the Great Fire of London, but little of it now dates back more than a hundred years or so. It lies on the site of old hunting grounds. "So ho!" was the shout that used to go up when the hunter spotted a quarry.

Soho's chief appeal these days is not its reputation for naughty night clubs – most are nothing more than tawdry – but its cheerful cosmopolitan character. Excellent continental restaurants, German and Scandinavian delicatessens, Italian bakers and French patisseries make it a delight for the gourmet.

Shaftesbury Avenue, at the southern end of Soho, leads back into Piccadilly Circus. Going west from there, along Piccadilly itself, there is much to see. On the left, almost immediately is a Wren Church, St James's, with some superb wood carvings by Grinling Gibbons, whose work graces many fine old houses and stately homes in southern England. Further along is Hatchards, one of London's leading booksellers; and Fortnum and Mason, the food emporium with delicacies from all over the world, is always worth a visit, though the shopper on a limited budget should proceed with caution. Linger, too, to watch the wall clock outside Fortnum's with its beautiful little figures that make an appearance every hour and half hour with the clock's chimes.

On to the other – the north – side of Piccadilly and look for Albany standing back in its own quiet little courtyard away from the hustle and bustle of Piccadilly. It is a

Pictured at the Royal Windsor Horse Show is the beautifully outfitted drum horse 'Cicero' left.

distinguished old house built at the end of the eighteenth century and now divided into exclusive apartments. One recent distinguished resident was Edward Heath, the former Prime Minister.

Further along is Burlington House, where the Royal Academy of Art stages major exhibitions, and Burlington Arcade, reputed to be the world's longest and oldest (opened in 1819) covered walk, lined by the most attractive little shops selling jewellery, militaria, perfume and examples of British craftsmanship such as woven tartan.

Down past Green Park tube station and Green Park itself laps up to the railings of Piccadilly on the South side. Here on Sunday mornings, amateur painters, from the talented to the merely enthusiastic, hang their latest masterpieces available for sale for as little as £5.

Before reaching Hyde Park Corner at the end of Piccadilly, dive down the narrow White Horse Street to the right and wander round a genuine London village – Shepherd Market, with its own distinct character formed by pavement cafés, several excellent restaurants, two or three extremely sociable pubs and some quaint little shops where personal service is the criterion of the proprietor.

Shepherd Market lies at the south end of Mayfair. Several elegant streets lead north into Grosvenor Square over which the massive eagle of the impressive American Embassy keeps beady-eyed watch. Continue north into Oxford Street but delay the shopping expedition there until you have walked up towards Marble Arch, where the Arch itself is sited close to the spot where the Tyburn Gallows dispatched many a villain in days gone by. For 600 years, until 1783, Londoners gathered here to watch public executions, a favourite form of entertainment. Cross over to the corner of Hyde Park where, if it's Sunday afternoon, you'll experience one of the great free entertainments London can offer – Speaker's Corner. Here, anyone can stand on his own soapbox, and speak publicly on any subject he likes. He or she will be assured of a big audience and a lot of good natured heckling. The Corner has its own "regular" speakers who are quite accomplished, and occasionally public figures will also come to speak, subject to the same heckling as any other. But they enter the spirit of the location, giving no quarter and expecting none.

Walk back along Oxford Street, allowing plenty of time to sample the wares of what is probably the city's major shopping street. Among the tried and tested attractions are general stores like Selfridges, Marks & Spencer, John Lewis, Marshall & Snelgrove, and, for music enthusiasts, the HMV record shop that caters for every music taste from classical to jazz, rock and punk. Continue along to Oxford Circus, then turn right into one of London's most classically elegant streets – Regent Street. It was originally designed by the architect John Nash to provide the Prince Regent, later George IV, with a direct route between his palace and Regent's Park, but little of the original conception remains. However, the curving sweep of the street is still impressive and some of the shops – Liberty and Dickins and Jones among them – are London's most sophisticated.

Holborn and Bloomsbury, lying about a mile to the east of Piccadilly Circus, are well worth a visit. Here the presence of business offices is more obvious than further west but this does not detract from the area. It gives W.C.1. (west central postal region) a character of its own. It contains many places of interest – the Inns of Court, the British Museum, the University of London and numerous pleasant walks through courtyards and narrow streets. The name Holborn is thought to derive from the old English word "Bourne" meaning river or stream. The original area was a low-lying tract of ground, a hole, near the old Fleet River which now runs underground north of Fleet Street. Just to the south of Holborn (the street) lies Lincoln's Inn, one of London's four Inns of Court, the others being Gray's Inn, and the Inner and Middle Temples. Here a lawyer learns his profession, usually as a member of chambers – a firm to whom he is articled or apprenticed. Law has been practised on the site of Lincoln's Inn since the thirteenth century; although nothing remains from that time, much of the existing architecture is Tudor. Like the other Inns, Lincoln's Inn has an air of unhurried calm and tranquillity about it. Benches are dotted about the little courtyards and paths for those requiring a period of quiet contemplation. The Inner and Middle Temples, just the other side of Fleet Street, were called by Charles Lamb "the most elegant spot in the metropolis" with their beautifully kept lawns and gardens. These inns were originally owned by the Crusading Knights Templars, hence the name, and there are still strong connections and traditions dating back to the time of the Crusades. Adjoining Lincoln's Inn are Lincoln's Inn Fields, a large open square, with tennis courts and expanses of grass, occupied during summer weekdays by office workers with their sandwiches, but at weekends a quiet oasis in the heart of the city.

Further down Holborn towards Holborn Circus, a turning to the left leads into Hatton Garden where diamond merchants, some in what now look like rundown premises, carry on their lucrative trade. And further along Holborn, across the viaduct that takes the road over what was the Fleet valley, lies Old Bailey, housing the Central Criminal Courts, where many of the most famous cases in the history of British justice have taken place. Earlier on this site stood the infamous Newgate Prison where public hangings were a frequent occurrence.

Retracing the way back along Holborn and then turning north at Southampton Row, Bloomsbury lies to the left. Bloomsbury is the literary centre of London where many publishers still have their offices. Much of the architecture is Georgian and the area is pinpointed with attractive squares and the two major sites of the British Museum and the University of London. Literary connections and associations are visible in almost every street with blue wall plaques indicating the reason. Disraeli lived in Bloomsbury as a young man and the so-called Bloomsbury Set, ruled by Virginia Woolf, held court there in the 1920s.

Dante Gabriel Rossetti lived in Red Lion Square and a

short distance away in Doughty Street Charles Dickens kept house for three years. It is now maintained as a museum and library open to the public.

To the south of Holborn lie the Strand (meaning "beach" which once it was to the Thames) and, where the City of London begins at Temple Bar, Fleet Street, the centre of the newspaper industry. Three major London theatres line the Strand, as well as some interesting shops, but a diversion to the north leads to Covent Garden, once the site of the famous vegetable market, now transported across the river to the Nine Elms site. Still in Covent Garden is the Inigo Jones church of St Paul's, set in the centre of a square which Shaw used for the opening scene in *Pygmalion*, later staged and filmed as *My Fair Lady*. Nearby is the Royal Opera House and the Theatre Royal, Drury Lane where *My Fair Lady* opened in London. A theatre has been on this site since 1663 but the present one dates from the early 1800s.

Between the Strand and the Thames is a pub called the Gilbert and Sullivan in John Adam Street (the area was built by the Adam brothers but little remains of their designs now). The pub has charming models of the operas dotted around its walls and mementos of W. S. Gilbert and Arthur Sullivan; very appropriate, because only a few hundred yards away, next to the famous hotel of the same name, is the Savoy Theatre where many of the original Gilbert and Sullivan operettas were first performed.

Towards the end of the Strand, and just before the Central Law Courts is the Aldwych, at which theatre the Royal Shakespeare Company has its London headquarters. And just beyond there is the church of St Clement Danes, built by Wren, which has been immortalised in the famous nursery rhyme, "Oranges and Lemons, say the bells of St Clements." Dr Johnson was a regular worshipper at the church, living a five-minute walk away in Gough Square – a turning to the left off Fleet Street leads to it. His house at no. 17 remains a fine example of Queen Anne architecture. Fleet Street itself now houses only two national newspapers, The Daily Telegraph and the Daily Express, but most of the others, as well as many provincial newspapers, have offices in the neighborhood.

The continuation of Fleet Street, Ludgate Hill, leads up past St Pauls and into the City of London proper. The "square mile", as it is known, stretches along the north bank of the Thames from Temple Bar to the Tower of London. It is governed by the Lord Mayor and his Court of Aldermen and even the Queen, traditionally, has to seek the Mayor's permission before entering. The City has its own police force and courts of law and during the working day upwards of half a million people earn their living there in the commercial heart of the capital. But by the weekend the City is populated by just 5,000 residents. Its street names indicate the trades and markets that used to flourish there – Bread Street (where John Milton was born), Wood Street, Ironmonger Lane and Poultry.

Near Bread Street, which runs into Cheapside, is the church of St Mary-le-Bow. To have been born within the sound of its bells – Bow Bells – is necessary for anyone who calls himself a cockney. And it was these same bells that summoned Dick Whittington back to become three times Lord Mayor, according to the legend.

Among the institutions in the City are the Mansion House, (the Lord Mayor's official residence), the Bank of England, the Monument designed by Wren to commemorate the Great Fire of London, the Royal Exchange (no longer in commercial use but once the market place for traders in agricultural produce), and the Guildhall where the Lord Mayor and his Sheriffs are elected. The first Guildhall was built in the early fifteenth century, but much of what can be seen now dates from the seventeenth century. Look for the memorials to two great Englishmen, Lord Nelson and Sir Winston Churchill, and the statues of two great figures of legend, Gog and Magog.

Just over the River lies the South Bank, redeveloped since World War Two and providing Londoners and visitors alike with a wealth of cultural possibilities. Nestling against Waterloo Bridge is the New National Theatre and within a few hundred yards are the National Film Theatre, the Hayward Gallery, which has a deserved reputation for presenting the best of new developments in art, and the Queen Elizabeth Hall, a concert hall specialising in chamber and ensemble music. Further along is the Royal Festival Hall, built to commemorate the 1951 Festival of Britain and now probably London's leading concert hall for orchestral and ballet works. Further on is the impressive County Hall, headquarters for the giant Greater London Council, the administrative body for the whole of London, apart from the City. Continuing the riverside walk, one comes to St Mary's Church tucked close beside the grandeur of Lambeth Palace. Here Captain Bligh – Bligh of the Bounty – is buried.

Lambeth Palace is the official residence of the Archbishops of Canterbury. The site dates back to the thirteenth century and landmarks of English ecclesiastical history are set there: the English prayer book was composed at Lambeth by Cranmer; conflicts of Church and State have taken place there and the evolution of the English Protestant Church has been planned and supervised there for centuries. It is not open to the public, except by appointment, but it is well worth a visit to ponder such affairs from the outside.

The walk along the South Bank, particularly when the Thames is in full spate, is a memorable experience. The skyline on the opposite, northern bank, with such profiles as St Pauls, Big Ben and the House of Commons clearly visible is truly impressive. A summer's evening there with London's lights beginning to flicker on is an ideal conclusion to a first visit to the city that Heinrich Heine once described as "the greatest wonder which the world can show to the astonished spirit".

A time exposure reduces the roar of London's traffic around the statue popularly known as Eros that in fact represents the Angel of Christian Charity, to a sea of color around its base overleaf.

DA UIRI RUM
LEMON
HART
RUM
e a Coke
ELICIOUS
REFRESHING
GUINNESS
TIME
WITH THE WINE
EMPIRE
AIR
CINZ
THE BIA
SKOL
International
LAGER
LONDONS LEADING JEWELLERS
H. SAMUEL

FACTOR
For Charm
ORDON'S
GIN
STANDS SUPREME
MON
CHÉRI
WRIGLEYS
SPEARMINT
healthful
delicious
satisfying
DAILY
EXPRESS
disci
EROS JEWELLERS
DRAUGHT
GUINNESS

Familiar red London buses cross Lambeth Bridge above against a background of the old London skyline.

Epitomizing the new London is the futuristic silhouette of the Post Office Tower top left which houses, in addition to a great deal of technological hardware, a revolving restaurant.

Probably one of the most familiar views of London by night is Piccadilly Circus center left, with its famous neon signs.

A festive touch is added to Trafalgar Square and its beautiful fountains by the erection of an illuminated Christmas tree below left, an annual gift from the people of Norway, and to Regent Street below, by gaily colored decorations suspended far above the heads of Christmas shoppers.

The imposing clock tower of Big Ben stands as a symbol of London above the night-time traffic in Whitehall right.

Impressive pageantry on display overleaf as the Horse Guards make their way down The Mall.

13

The broad sweep of Whitehall is shown above left *with, in the foreground, the tall column of the Cenotaph, commemorating those who fell in two world wars.*

An oasis for the weary sightseer is provided above by the cooling waters of the lakes and fountains of Trafalgar Square.

The Albert Hall *center left is a popular venue for all manner of entertainments, ranging from symphonic concerts to boxing matches.*

On the south bank of the Thames, next to Westminster Bridge, stands London County Hall *below left, with its extensive river frontage.*

Below is shown the classical building that houses the Port of London Authority *and* right *the west front of Westminster Abbey.*

Buckingham Palace *overleaf has been the London home of Britain's sovereigns since 1837.*

Although the world famous clock which is featured on these pages is affectionately known as Big Ben, this name is a misnomer. The structure, standing by the House of Commons is, in fact, The Clock Tower and Big Ben is the name given to the bell it houses, in honor of the first Commissioner of Works, Sir Benjamin Hall.

Nevertheless the clock, symbolizing so much – to the people of London particularly, and to the whole country in general – will continue to be known as Big Ben.

The winged and gilded figure overleaf stands atop the Victoria Memorial in Queen's Gardens, in front of Buckingham Palace.

Great Buildings

FOR a city whose history goes back nearly 2,000 years London has a fine display of great buildings, but because of the devastation of the Great Fire and two world wars, few of them date back further than the seventeenth century. Nevertheless they are elegant examples of the finest architecture of their period which, combined with the people and events in their history, give them great popular appeal.

St Pauls: One of the most familiar landmarks on the London skyline, Wren's cathedral is, in fact, the fifth church on the site; the first was built as long ago as the seventh century. Work started on the current version under Wren's direction in 1675 and was completed 35 years later, by which time Wren was 78. But he lived on for another 13 years, was a regular worshipper there and is now buried in the Crypt with the touchingly apt inscription: "If you seek this man's monument, look around you." The tombs of Lord Nelson and the Duke of Wellington are also to be found there, as well as alcoves in memory of musicians and writers, soldiers and sailors. Another chapel is dedicated to "the American dead of the Second World War from the people of Britain" and contains a showcase in which is a handwritten volume listing the names of all those who died during the last war. The dome of St Pauls soars 220 feet and is an inspiring sight with scenes from the life of St Paul depicted on it; and on the way up children and adults alike are ever fascinated by the whispering gallery whose rounded walls will carry the quietest of conversations round from one side to the other.

Tower of London: Steeped in history, the Tower has performed many roles, among them that of fortress (under the Normans), place of execution and torture (under the Tudors), palace, miniature zoo (Henry III kept a small menagerie there, including, so the story goes, a polar bear tethered on a piece of rope long enough to allow the animal to plop into the Thames for the occasional bite of fresh fish), and museum – which is the service it performs today. The White Tower is the oldest part, built by William I from whitish stone brought from Normandy by the Normans. It walls, 15 feet thick in places, were meant to, and did, resist attack. It now houses the impressive national arms museum. The rest of the Tower is medieval, with Traitors Gate and the Bloody Tower the best known features. It was at the sight of the Gate 400 years ago that Good Queen Bess, Elizabeth I of England, broke down and wept as she passed through after her sister Mary had banished her to the Tower. And it was in the Bloody Tower that the two young princes, Edward V and Richard of York, were murdered in 1483. Their bodies lay hidden for nearly 200 years until a workmen's pick uncovered them and they were reburied in Westminster Abbey. Walking from the Bloody Tower to the White Tower you pass Tower Green where many executions took place, notably those of Anne Boleyn, Catherine Howard and Lady Jane Grey. The Crown Jewels are also housed in the Tower but most of them are not as old as people think. Many of the original Jewels were destroyed by Cromwell and those on view today date from the Restoration when Charles II had the Jewels replaced. The two highlights of the collection are undoubtedly the Black Prince's ruby, thought to have been worn by Henry V at Agincourt in 1415 and now set in the Crown of State; and the famous Koh-i-noor diamond (the name means mountain of light) set in the crown that was made for the 1937 coronation of Queen Elizabeth, the Queen Mother.

Westminster Abbey: The Abbey, officially the Collegiate Church of St Peter, is where most British monarchs are crowned and buried. The Cathedral, more than 500 feet long, is really in three sections – Edward the Confessor's Shrine, Henry VII's Chapel and the Commoners' Abbey. The royal tombs – among them Elizabeth I, Henry V, Mary Queen of Scots, Anne, Richard II – lie behind the altars in Edward's Shrine and Henry's Chapel, and in the former, too, is the Coronation Chair that dates back to Edward I, with the famous Stone of Scone that has been a bone of contention between the English and the more fervent Scottish nationalists for centuries, culminating in its removal from the Abbey in 1950 (no mean feat in itself because it is extremely heavy) and eventual recovery north of the border. Henry's chapel was originally to be dedicated to his father after he had been canonized, but the Pope asked too high a sum for the dedication, so Henry changed his mind and had the chapel dedicated to himself. Poets' Corner features memorials to such great names as Chaucer, Shakespeare, Tennyson, Milton and Longfellow, and by the great west door is the famous tomb of the unknown warrior, whose body was brought back from France after the First World War.

Houses of Parliament: Apart from the majestic and echoing St. Stephens Hall which dates back to 1097, most of what can now be seen is no older than 140 years. It was designed in the perpendicular style after the disastrous 1834 fire which gutted the Commons, by Sir Charles Barry who was also responsible for designing Tower Bridge. The Palace of Westminster, as it is known, covers eight acres and has nearly two miles of corridors with more than 1,000 mainly small and overcrowded rooms opening off them. Even the Chamber of the Commons, where Parliament conducts its business is, to the first time visitor, surprisingly small; and when the Chamber is crowded for an important debate MPs sit literally cheek by jowl on the open benches. When Parliament is sitting the fact is confirmed by the Union Jack flying on the Victoria Tower during the day, and at night by the light in the clock tower of Big Ben. St Stephens Hall contains what is thought to be the finest timbered roof in Europe – built from Sussex oak by Richard II in 1399. It has been restored in part from time to time, on each occasion with oak from the same wood, supplied by descendants of the original suppliers.

Buckingham Palace: Until 1913 the Palace ran round three sides of a courtyard, but the fourth side, the part of the building the public now sees, was added in 1913. It was originally built in 1703 for the Duke of Buckingham who later sold it to George II for the princely sum of £21,000. The public rarely sees inside either palace or the attractive 40-acre gardens; the only regular access is to the Queen's Gallery where a selection of the Queen's superb art collection is displayed, or to the Royal Mews where the Royal coaches are stored. Chief among them is the Golden State Coach used for every coronation since George IV and, as are all the coaches, lovingly maintained by the Mews staff. The carriage horses, Cleveland Bays and Windsor Greys, are also stabled in the Mews, adjoining the harness room where the eye is caught by the glittering brasswork on such exhibits as George IV's saddle and the hand-made pony harnesses that generations of royal children have used.

London is far more than a collection of historic buildings, grand hotels, such as Claridge's left, or world renowned establishments like Sotheby's below. It is a thriving community of ordinary people, with street markets selling goods ranging from fresh fruit and vegetables, the latest in cut-price crockery to the assorted knick-knacks and antiques that may be found in the Portobello Road Market overleaf.

25

BRITISH FARM EGGS

Wren's masterpiece, St Paul's Cathedral, still excites the imagination. Designed to dominate the London of the 17th century, its sheer beauty and majesty still compare favorably with any of the more recent buildings built in the vicinity.

Dominating Westminster is Westminster Abbey overleaf.

Wearing their traditional scarlet coats and proudly displaying their campaign medals are some of the veterans of the Chelsea Royal Hospital. The hospital, which was designed by Sir Christopher Wren, was founded for retired and invalid soldiers by Charles II in 1682.

Three of the bridges that span London's River Thames are pictured overleaf. Top is Chelsea Bridge, center the Albert Bridge and bottom the rather more modern Waterloo Bridge.

Parks

THE one characteristic of London that never fails to draw compliments from visitors is the extent of parkland in the centre of the city. In fact, there are more than 1200 acres of green spaces, trees, spring bulbs, and lakes within central London where it is possible to feel genuinely in the country. The noise of traffic is reduced to nothing more than a distant murmur and competes only with the buzz of summer insects to keep the visitor awake in his deckchair. In the warmer months office workers take their lunchtime sandwiches into the parks and, in the general English pursuit of the elusive sun, take any opportunity to improve their suntans. But they stay on the fringes; in the depths of Hyde Park or particularly Regents Park it is possible to find tranquil isolation with only the finches, blackbirds and squirrels for company.

Pitt the Elder, the English statesman, described the city's parks as "the lungs of London"; the air certainly seems to smell fresher there.

The Central London parks – St James's, Green, Hyde and Kensington Gardens – provide a marvellous opportunity for a 3-mile country walk in the heart of the city. Starting from the Admiralty Arch side of St James's Park, cross in front of Buckingham Palace into Green Park; then head towards Hyde Park Corner and in to Hyde Park walking the length of its before entering Kensington Gardens. It is a delightful walk in which you need only encounter road traffic twice.

St James's Park is in fact the oldest of the Royal Parks. It was largely bog and marsh until Henry VIII had it cleared of water and stocked it with deer for hunting. More than a century later Charles II brought over to England the French landscape designer, Le Notre, famous for his work at Versailles, and commissioned him to lay out a new St James's. He allowed for a lake, islands, an aviary (hence Birdcage Walk) and, on the King's instructions, a long stretch of level ground on which Charles could play his great passion – the French game of *paille maille*. The game has long since died out, but the name lives on alongside St James's Park, as Pall Mall. Charles also introduced various species of birds to the islands in the five-acre lake and today this area is a sanctuary with many kinds of duck, as well as more exotic birds such as pelicans.

Green Park's 53 acres make it the smallest of the Royal Parks but with its wooded slopes and the occasional grazing sheep it has a particular charm of its own. It once was a favourite duelling spot.

Hyde Park is perhaps the most famous of the London parks. It is a favourite place for Londoners at weekends and Bank Holidays with the Serpentine offering swimming and boating on its tranquil but cold waters. The site was one of Henry VIIIs hunting grounds and it also ran up to the infamous gallows of Tyburn (roughly where Marble Arch now stands). When Charles II came to the throne, he had the bodies of Cromwell and other Roundheads removed from their tombs in Westminster Abbey and symbolically hanged from Tyburn. A plaque records this grim event at Marble Arch.

In William III's time, Hyde Park had become notorious for footpads and felons preying on innocent passers-by. The King, who was an asthma sufferer, had moved out to the cleaner air at Kensington Palace, and decided to cut a route through Hyde Park up to the Palace, hung with lamps to keep the villains away. It became known as the *Route du Roi*, the King's way which, it is thought, is the derivation of Rotten Row where later Victorian and Edwardian gentlemen wooed their ladies on horseback.

Hyde Park, too, was a duelling site, the most famous of which was the encounter between Lord Mohun and the Duke of Hamilton. The Duke pierced the Lord's guard and as Mohun lay dying, the Duke bent over him to administer comfort. In his dying breath, Mohun thrust upward with his sword and both men died within minutes of each other.

These days, the Park is more peaceful; the occasional game of soccer gets a little heated, and expatriate Americans who gather many Sunday mornings for some nostalgia with a game of baseball, are also prone to excitement.

Beyond Hyde Park going west is Kensington Gardens, where Queen Victoria was brought up as a child. In the heart of exclusive Belgravia, it has been a favourite haunt of nannies with their charges whose childhoods revolved around the famous Peter Pan statue worn smooth at the base by thousands of admiring hands; and there's the Round Pond, which attracts model boat enthusiasts by the convoy.

The other major central park is Regents Park, another former Royal hunting ground that was designed by Nash for the Prince Regent and which now with its big lake, children's pond, running tracks, sports fields and London Zoo nearby runs Hyde Park close as a recreational centre. It also has Queen Mary's Rose Garden and the Open Air Theatre where, in good weather, fine Shakespeare productions can be enjoyed in what is almost a natural amphitheatre.

Further north are the wild open spaces of Hampstead Heath where at holiday time funfairs abound and where, from the adjoining Spaniards Road, with its beautiful but usually crowded old Spaniard's Inn, superb views can be had as far as the Surrey and Kent Hills.

London also has its small intimate public gardens, too numerous to list here. They can be stumbled upon most unexpectedly and are all the better for that. Usually immaculately maintained by the local authority, with manicured lawns and flower beds that seem to be a riot of colour all the year round, they also sometimes contain the ultimate compliment to their existence. On the occasional bench will be a plaque donated at the dying request of one who "spent many pleasant hours in the evening of his life" in the peace of a London garden.

Pictured from Trafalgar Square, Admiralty Arch overleaf *marks the entrance to The Mall, the long, broad avenue that leads to Buckingham Palace.*

As might be expected London can provide, for those so inclined, elegant living and dining. There are traditional hotels with all the grace, dignity and style that their names and ages imply, and there are modern establishments. All, however, can supply accommodation and cuisine of a very high standard indeed. Left, right and below: *Inn on the Park*. Above: the *Dorchester-Penthouse Restaurant*.

Between Hyde Park and Green Park, which together make up London's largest open space, lies Hyde Park Corner overleaf on which stands Constitution Arch.

If it is intended to eat in style, there could hardly be a better way to start than by pulling up at the door of the chosen hotel in that most elegant of cars, the Rolls Royce above and to be met by, in this case, the doorman of the Intercontinental. The photograph left was taken in the International's restaurant.

Once inside the hotel's restaurant it becomes apparent that the decor and, in particular, the cuisine, fully meet expectations. The variety and presentation of the various dishes are of a very high standard and there is, almost invariably, a speciality of the house to be sampled. Above, left, below and right: the Sheraton Park Tower.

A flower seller sits in the sunshine, waiting for customers overleaf left and right; a display of blooms on a hand cart creates a blaze of color in the city's streets.

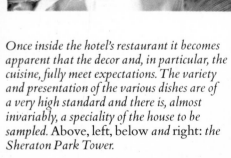

Gambling has long been an integral part of the night-life of most big cities, and London is no exception. In gaming rooms such as these, huge sums of money may be won or lost at the turn of a card or the spin of a wheel. No doubt the really serious gamblers would find any distraction an intrusion into their concentration but most of the clientèle appreciate the presence of pretty girls to help the evening along. Below is pictured the Claremont Club. All other pictures show the Playboy Club.

The Wheatsheaf public house overleaf is an old hostelry, typical of many still to be found in the metropolis. This one is situated in Rathbone Place, near the junction of Oxford Street and Tottenham Court Road.

Museums and Art Galleries

THE British may not have produced the world's leading artists but they have a reputation second to none as collectors of *objêts d'art*. During Britain's great era as a colonial power, her explorers brought back a wealth of antiquities which are now displayed for public viewing in the nation's museums and galleries, many of which are in London. Much of the world's fine art comes to London for sale at the internationally famous auction houses of Sotheby's and Christie's and some of it finds its way into those same institutions, the most impressive of which must be:

The British Museum: this formidable building with its sweeping façade looking out over Great Russell Street draws visitors from around the world. It is a treasure trove of prints, drawings, Greek, Roman, Egyptian, Oriental and British relics, coins, medals and original documents. Among many outstanding exhibits are the Rosetta Stone and Elgin Marbles, the statues and friezes brought back at huge expense from Athens in 1803 by Lord Elgin. There is the amazingly preserved body of an Egyptian believed to have lived 3500 years before Christ. It was found in a grave beneath the Sahara sands which had sealed it against deterioration. In the manuscript room are the final words written by the antarctic explorer Scott before he died a few miles from the South Pole: "For God's sake, look after our people." And there is Lewis Carroll's original manuscript for *Alice in Wonderland.* Apart from the Museum, there is the renowned Library where many famous scholars have carried out their researches; Karl Marx had a regular seat there. The Library inherited the Sloane collection, some 50,000 books and 4,000 manuscripts, which provided the basis for the establishment of the British Museum back in 1759.

The Kensington museums – the Victoria and Albert, the Science Museum, the Natural History Museum and the Geological Museum – all sited within a mile or so of each other – provide a feast of exhibits. The V & A, as it is affectionately known, specialises in fine and applied arts. Costumes, furnishings and musical instruments, many of a bizarre kind, are to be found there. The Great Bed of Ware that sleeps eight, and was immortalised by Shakespeare in *Twelfth Night,* is one of the major attractions. And Tipu's Tiger, a working model that shows a man-eating tiger enjoying a human meal, has fascinated generations of children. The Natural History Museum has remarkable reconstructions of huge prehistoric beasts, a huge 90-foot model of the giant Blue Whale and a model of the legendary dodo that has been extinct since 1693. The Science Museum with its great variety of press-button working models is a must for parents and their children. Among the exhibits here are Puffing Billy, the world's oldest locomotive, Stephenson's Rocket of 1829, the first powered flight machine of the Wright brothers and Spitfires and Hurricanes from World War Two, as well as more recent items such as a recreation of the Apollo Moon landing in 1969.

The Museum of London at London Wall has virtually every important relic unearthed from beneath the city to depict its 2,000-year history. There's a Roman legionary's armour, Danish battle axes more than 800 years old, remains from the Fire of London alongside an early fire engine, and colourful recreations of the interior of a Roman house, of a Newgate prison cell and the original London Bridge.

Covering a similar period of history but concentrating on the more macabre episodes is the London Dungeon situated in creepy vaults beneath London Bridge Station. Here are grim exhibits from the Plague, recreations of Tyburn hangings, a Druid sacrifice and tortures at the Tower, all made the more nightmarish by the dank, candlelit atmosphere.

The Imperial War Museum in Lambeth Road commemorates the two World Wars with a huge range of memontos, documents, paintings, photographs, films, guns, tanks and aircraft. Here one can see the original 1945 document of German surrender, Field Marshal Montgomery's campaign caravan, doodlebugs (the German V1 rockets), a Spitfire and a Mosquito… And there are vivid recreations of scenes from World War One – the trenches, a recruiting room and a troop train.

The major art galleries include the National in Trafalgar Square which features the best of British painting as well as a comprehensive collection of European masters of the past 500 years; the Royal Academy in Piccadilly, the home of traditional painting; the Tate at Millbank with a fine collection of Turners and Blakes, as well as French impressionists; the Hayward Gallery near the Festival Hall, London's leading modern gallery; and the Institute of Contemporary Arts Gallery in Carlton House Terrace which provides display space for experimental forms – "happenings", spectator participation and the like.

And in a lighter vein there are a myriad of smaller collections such as the Bethnal Green Museum, a superb display of dolls, toys and dolls houses including some beautiful Victorian working models; there's Dickens House at 48 Doughty Street where the writer lived until 1839 and where now are housed portraits, letters, autographs and some of the furniture he used.

And although not a museum, the collection of wax models at Mme Tussauds on Marylebone Road demands a visit. This exhibit has been in London since 1802 when Mme Tussaud fled persecution in her native Paris following the French Revolution. Just about every major figure in public life is there in lifelike pose – the British Prime Minister, American Presidents from Washington to Carter, Queen Elizabeth, Prince Charles, Winston Churchill, Muhammed Ali, Rudolf Nureyev and so on. In the Chamber of Horrors, a range of gruesome exhibits includes such evil characters as Robespierre, Crippen and the assassin of President Kennedy.

London, then, has much to offer the visitor in its museums and galleries, most of which make no admission charge. For the collector or student of history, a complete holiday could be spent in them economically and entertainingly.

The large, open space that is Trafalgar Square, with its lakes and fountains and its statue of the victor of the Battle of Trafalgar, Lord Nelson, makes an impressive sight, particularly when bathed in the glow of floodlighting overleaf.

Visitors to London from all over the world
invariably express a wish to attend one or
other of London's many fine theatres. First
class entertainment – whether a
performance of one of Shakespeare's works,
a modern play, a musical, ballet or
opera – is assured.
The theatres pictured on these pages show
Wyndhams *top left, the* Windmill *above,*
St Martin's *and the* Ambassador
top right, the Aldwych *center right, the*
Palladium *bottom right,* Covent
Garden *below and the original home of
the hit musical 'Jesus Christ – Superstar'*
below left.

Overleaf *is depicted another famous
London entertainments centre, the*
Royal Festival Hall.

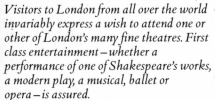

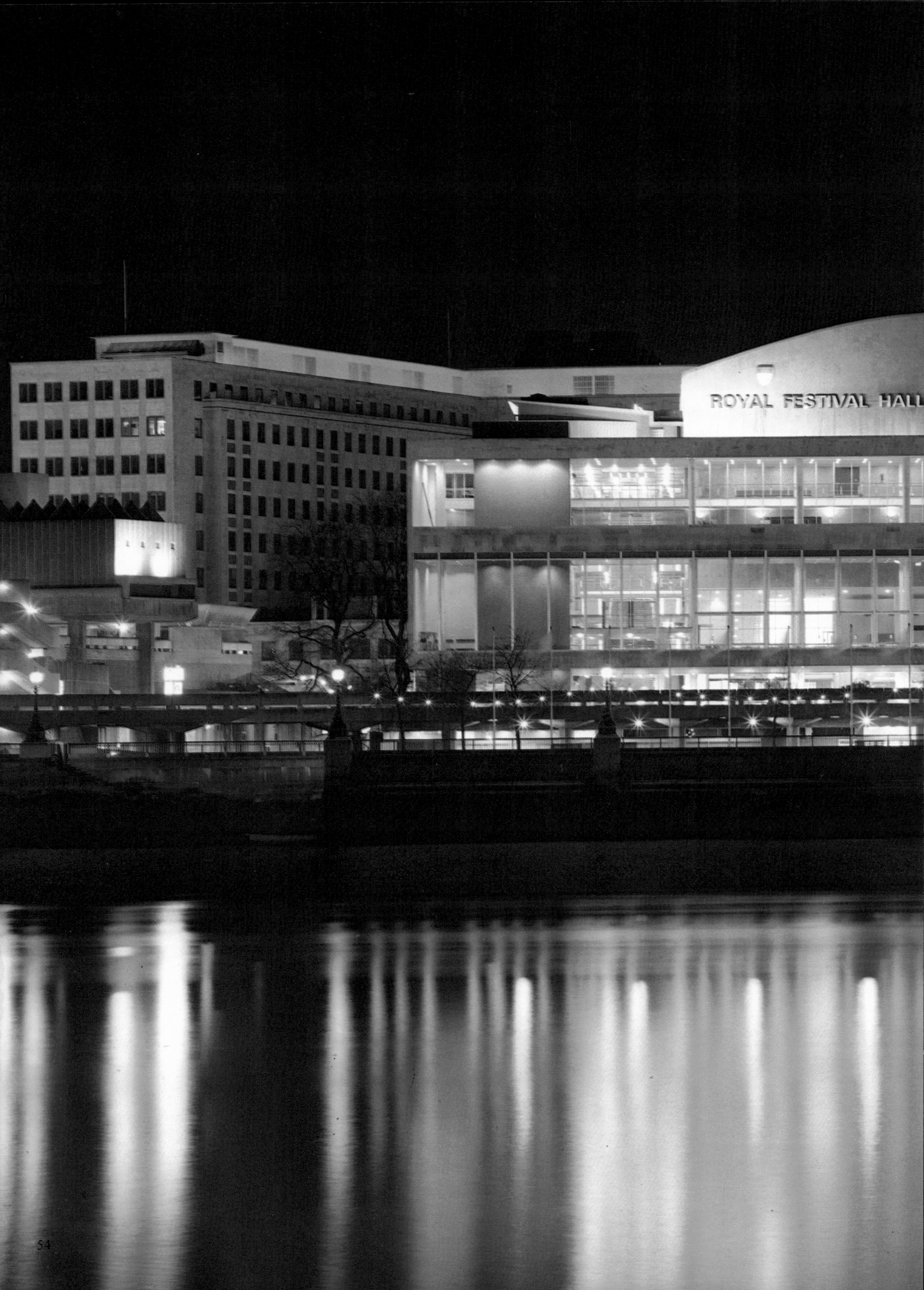
ROYAL FESTIVAL HALL

Ballet brings together four distinct and separate art forms; those of music, dancing, drama and painting. It can trace its origins back to the days of classical Greece but the art form as we know it today developed in France, at the Court of King Louis XIV. London is the home of the two major National Companies – those of the Festival Ballet and the Company of the Royal Ballet.
In addition to the resident companies there are often performances by visiting dancers. One such celebrated visitor, Rudolf Nureyev, pictured right, decided some years ago to make his home in England and he has proved a welcome and colorful addition to the London ballet scene.

The unusual view overleaf of the interior of St Paul's Cathedral was taken from the famous 'Whispering Gallery' and provides an excellent indication of the scale of Wren's masterpiece.

Very few buildings in the world can have witnessed so much of a country's history as the solid and uncompromising Tower of London pages 60 – 61.

Entertainment

FOR sheer diversity of entertainment and culture London can claim to be the world's leading city. In concert hall, theatre, cinema, club and pub every taste is catered for; and the professional performances in most are unrivalled anywhere for quality and style.

To underline the variety of entertainment available, here is a brief selection of what one could see on just one night chosen at random: a performance of *La Bohème* by the English National Opera Company; the renowned Chicago Symphony Orchestra at a Royal Albert Hall Promenade Concert; a Royal Shakespeare Company production of *As You Like It;* a Tom Stoppard play; the Black African musical *Ipi Tombi;* musicals *Jesus Christ Superstar, Evita* and *Elvis* and – still – Agatha Christie's *The Mousetrap,* the world's longest running production, now in its 26th year.

There are altogether over 60 theatres to choose from, with the work of some of the world's leading dramatists, directors and players on show. The doyen of London theatres must surely be the Old Vic, originally a gin palace, converted into the Royal Victorian Music Hall and then, from 1912 when the legendary Lilian Baylis took over, committed to producing live theatre for the man in the street at prices he could afford. From the Old Vic came the Royal Shakespeare Company, now housed elsewhere, the Royal Ballet Company, the English National Opera and, more recently, the National Theatre. The English cultural heritage owes Miss Baylis and the Old Vic a great debt.

The British cinema industry is only a shadow of its former self, but there are nevertheless nearly 100 cinemas in London, some with as many as five small separate auditoria to enable five different films to be shown at the same time.

The musical scene is as healthy and varied as the live theatre. The Royal Festival Hall complex, opened in 1951 as part of the Festival of Britain celebrations, has three halls: the Festival Hall itself for orchestral concerts and ballet productions; the Queen Elizabeth Hall for chamber music and the intimate Purcell Room for solo recitals and, occasionally, folk music. The ornate but loveable Royal Albert Hall stages a variety of musical events throughout the year, reaching a climax with the Sir Henry Wood Promenade Concerts ending in September, at which many of the world's leading conductors, orchestras and soloists appear. The final night is a British institution with the Promenaders, many of whom have queued for nights outside to ensure a standing place in the central arena, good naturedly heckling the conductor, waving banners and placards, throwing streamers and singing with great gusto such traditional British music as the Sea Shanties and Parry's Jerusalem. Many a patriotic tear is shed that night.

There are open air concerts at Kenwood House and Holland Park, major operatic productions at Covent Garden (the Royal Opera Company) and the Coliseum (English National Opera); and five London ballet companies, led by the Royal Ballet which shares Covent Garden with the Royal Opera Company.

Jazz is alive and well in London, living mainly at the Ronnie Scott Club in Frith Street, Soho, where a regular stream of major American performers play two-week engagements, as well as the best British and European artists. Ronnie Scott himself lends an idiosyncratic contribution to most evenings with his inimitable brand of repartee.

Gambling and gaming is well catered for with a host of clubs, the most aristocratic of which is Crockfords. In elegant surroundings, thousands are quickly won and lost every night and many celebrities and well known businessmen can be seen there.

London provides a wide variety of restaurants – French, Italian, Greek, Scandinavian, Chinese, Indian, Japanese, Jewish and so on. But it is perhaps the pubs that visitors from abroad find so appealingly and uniquely British. There are estimated to be at least 5,000 in London and the choice is bewildering. The answer is to go with a Londoner to his local; but failing that, selection can be made on the basis of interest: historical pubs (for instance, Ye Olde Cheshire Cheese just off Fleet Street); riverside pubs (The City Barge at Chiswick); newspaper pubs (El Vinos winebar in Fleet Street), theatrical pubs (The Salisbury in St Martin's Lane) or tourist interest (Gilbert & Sullivan just off the Strand). British beer may be a little too warm for some tastes but the sociable and companiable atmosphere of the British pub is hard to beat.

The River and waterways of the capital are also a source of entertainment. Moored alongside the Thames are old ships like *HMS Discovery,* Scott's ship on his ill-fated Antarctic expedition; the 1860 tea clipper, the *Cutty Sark,* and the World War Two cruiser, *HMS Belfast.* Waterbuses stop at intervals along the Thames from Greenwich to Richmond and Hampton Court and a morning spent cruising up the river is a most enjoyable experience. There are canal trips, starting mainly from the picturesque Little Venice on Regents Canal near the Park, one of which takes its passengers straight to London Zoo.

Here one can spend a delightful day among the nearly 7,000 animals, birds and reptiles, let alone the huge collection of insects. The two Giant Pandas are among the star attractions – Ching-Ching (the lady's name, meaning Crystal Light) and Chia-Chia (Most Excellent, the gentleman) – along with the big monkeys, giraffes and sea-lions, penguins and walruses. There's no need to take food for the animals – they are well enough fed already. More than £150,000 is spent on their food each year. Apart from the huge quantities of staple foods such as eggs and potatoes, the ant-eaters have to have their ants, the reindeer specially imported lichen, and the flamingoes need cockles and shrimps to keep them pink.

And if sport is your entertainment, a day at the home of English cricket, Lords, will appeal even if you know nothing about the game. The bars are open all day and the crowd will keep you entertained. There's tennis at Wimbledon in June which, apart from being the world's leading tournament, is a considerable social occasion. You can hire horses for riding in Hyde Park, Richmond Park or Wimbledon Common; hire a boat or go for a swim in the Serpentine, or plunge in to any one of the many municipal swimming pools in the city.

There really is no excuse for not knowing what to do with one's time in London.

...wer Bridge left *was designed to blend with the medieval structure ...he Tower of London* above. *Despite its appearance, the bridge ...es only from the Victorian era, while the Tower's history spans ...ost nine centuries.*

...1 the other side of Tower Bridge, and adjacent to the Tower of ...ndon, lies St Katherine's Yacht Haven below left.

...stminster Abbey is shown right *as dusk falls, and the evening ...* accentuates the Gothic tracery of the Houses of ...rliament* below.

...e flowing form of a modern sculpture contrasts with the solid ...gularity of Tower Bridge overleaf.

Historic London

LONDON evolved as two entirely separate towns – the walled fortress founded by the Romans about AD 43 and the settlement that grew around the site of Westminster Abbey some 900 years later, the two separated by no more than a mile or two of marshy ground.

The Roman town developed after they forded the Thames between the gravel banks of what is now Ludgate Hill on the north bank and Southwark on the south, to allow their troops and transport, landing on the Kentish coast, access to their chief city, Colchester, to the north east and their further flung outposts to the north and west. Within a few years this crossing point became the hub of Roman activities in Britain, with Watling Street serving it from the south, running on north along the line of what is now the Edgware Road to St. Albans and eventually to the border country where Hadrian left his famous mark on the landscape: and other roads leading from it to feed Chichester, Silchester, Lincoln and York.

Under the Emperor Constantius, whose wife was a Briton, London flourished and at the beginning of the 3rd century AD its citizens enjoyed a standard of living that, according to historians, was not attained again until nearly 1500 years later. But it was shortlived, as was the Roman presence in Britain, and with the legions' departure the country under the Angles, Saxons and Jutes reverted to a farming economy; London was largely abandoned.

The Norman William was good for London: he rebuilt its fortifications, added the castle (now the part of the Tower known as the White Tower), had another church built on the St Paul's site (later to be destroyed by fire) and perhaps most importantly, granted a charter to the merchants of the city which laid down a measure of independence for it that the City still enjoys today in certain respects. The merchants were not slow to exercise this independence when they met at St Pauls to appoint Prince John Regent to Richard I in place of Richard's own choice whom they disliked. But John had to pay a price: in 1192 he established the city as a municipal corporation with its own mayor, later to be dignified as the Lord Mayor – an extremely influential position. Even today it is laid down that the Lord Mayor is among the first to be officially informed of a monarch's death and is traditionally the first to be summoned to a meeting of the Privy Council that announces the monarch's successor.

Just twenty years later, the City had had enough of John and forced him to sign the Magna Carta which said specifically of the capital: "Let the City of London have all its old liberties and its free customs, as well by land as by water."

Business continued to dominate London life and not even the Black Death, from which 50,000 died and were alleged to have been buried in the "smooth-field" (the site of Smithfield), seriously halted progress. The Guildhall was completed in 1425 and by Tudor times Smithfield and Cheapside were two of Europe's chief markets where, for instance, German clocks, French wines and Venetian glassware were sold alongside British cloth.

With the arrival of Henry VIII on the throne, Westminster's destiny was uprooted. He moved the court out of Westminster Palace in favour of the Palace of Whitehall, formerly the London residence of the Archbishops of York. And with the dissolution of the monasteries Westminster Abbey became a protestant church and St Stephens Hall the home of the Commons.

By the time the first Elizabeth was on the throne the combined population of London and Westminster was around 300,000, living largely in cramped dirty accommodation, made no better by sewage that constantly ran down the streets from the overflowing Fleet River. This, and the continual demolition and rebuilding of these times, led to a steady stream of removals from the City to Westminster and the land between, but it was war, the Civil War of Roundheads and Cavaliers, that finally brought the unification of London and Westminster into the largest city in Europe. Earthworks were built as defence against the Royalist troops, stretching from the Tower in the east, running parallel between the Fleet and the Thames, and around the Palace of Westminster.

Twenty years later the old London disappeared, first in the Plague which accounted for more than 50,000 lives, then in the Great Fire of 1666 which burned for four days, demolished 13,000 dwellings and left 200,000 homeless, many of them camped in the open outside the city walls.

But it gave the city fathers an opportunity which Sir Christopher Wren grasped for the redesigning of London and although his first imaginative plan was turned down on the grounds of cost, a new London started to emerge, part of which was St Pauls, finally completed in 1710. London now stretched into Bloomsbury, and, after King William moved the court to St James's Palace, into the area north of the Palace called Piccadilly. The Strand area between London and Westminster was elegantly developed by the Adams brothers; Soho and Regent Street were put on the map and the Fleet River was covered over and condemned to an underground existence. By the early nineteenth century the Georgian era was leaving a beauty mark on the face of London: the work of Nash adorned Regent Street and Buckingham Palace into which Victoria moved on her accession, after George III bought it from the Buckingham family.

The railway reached London in 1836 and, with its rapid development, suburbia and the commuter arrived. People were able to live outside the traditional square mile and the West End, as it came to be known, and still travel reasonably cheaply and comfortably to work.

The First World War gave London a taste of aerial warfare but it was not until 1940 that the true effects were felt when hundreds of enemy rockets and bombers filled the London sky. In those dark years, 29,000 Londoners died, 240,000 houses were destroyed and major damage was caused to such buildings as Buckingham Palace, the House of Commons and Westminster Abbey. Nearly half the city's churches were devastated. The cost of re-building was terrifying and it took London nearly twenty years to obliterate most of the scars – the bomb sites that once littered the city.

Facing the Royal Albert Hall is the Albert Memorial left, which was erected in 1876 in memory of the Prince Consort. It features a statue of the prince, under a Gothic canopy.
One of the loveliest of London's parks is St James's Park, pictured overleaf in the early Spring, when the daffodils are in bloom.

London's parks, gardens, squares and open spaces provide a welcome respite for resident and visitor alike. The Pagoda in Kew Gardens is pictured *left, the statue of the ever-youthful Peter Pan is shown* above *and lunch-time entertainment is provided in St James's Park by a military band* right. *The schoolgirls* top right *were photographed just off Sloane Street and the gentleman taking his leisure* below *in Hyde Park.*

The view toward Whitehall overleaf was taken from St James's Park.

Shops and Markets

UNLIKE most cities, London does not have one central shopping area. There are high quality shops and department stores in the West End, Knightsbridge and Chelsea, for instance, and time spent in all three can be equally rewarding.

In the West End, the main shopping streets are Piccadilly, Regent Street and Oxford Street. Selfridges is the major store in the latter, situated at the Marble Arch end. It has a superb food hall, a big household section, an excellent book department and fashion floors. At Christmas its windows are usually based on a children's theme, *Alice in Wonderland* for instance, and its children's department stocks just about every possible present.

The ever popular Marks & Spencer is next door, with another branch the other side of Oxford Circus, and a little further down the road on the other side is the excellent music shop, HMV, catering for all tastes, whether on record or tape. The John Lewis store, specialising in dress and furnishing fabrics, lies on the left as you approach Oxford Circus, and there are also the reputable stores of Bourne & Hollingsworth, D H Evans and Marshal & Snelgrove.

Turn right at the Circus into Regent Street and a triumvirate of stores faces you – Dickins & Jones, excellent for fabrics and costume jewellery, Jaeger for stylish woollens, and the timbered facade of Liberty that specialises in silks, clothes and prints. Further down on the left is Hamleys, one of the oldest and best of London's toyshops with each floor arranged according to age group and kind of toy. In Piccadilly, Fortnum and Mason is a must, selling exotic foods from around the world, as well as having floors devoted to gifts, high fashion and shirts and sweaters. Stop off, too, at Simpsons of Piccadilly for sportwear and at Hatchards, one of Londons best bookshops with particularly good children's and travel departments.

Knightsbridge is perhaps the most fashionable area of London and it has two stores that reflect that image: Harvey Nichols, with very chic lines in household accessories and fashions, and the prestigious Harrods, where just about anything can be bought or obtained (its telegraphic address is "Everything, London"). It has about 200 different departments and one of its busiest is the tourist bureau that handles the export of goods to foreign buyers. Harrods staff are handpicked for their education, courtesy and tact at all times. There's a superb sports department where sports celebrities and coaches are frequently on hand to offer advice. Harrods really is in a class of its own.

Kings Road running into the heart of Chelsea has a more Bohemian look to it, but there are still major stores like Peter Jones (a branch of John Lewis) with the same specialities. Don't miss the Chelsea Antique Market which usually has more than 100 stalls with bargains to be picked up in Victorian jewellery, among other things.

If antiques are on the agenda then it is worth visiting Church Street in Kensington which has some delightful little shops and St Christopher Place, a narrow alley opening off Oxford Street, that runs into an old building converted into little booths, each one specialising in different objects.

For china, glass and porcelain, the Wedgwood shop in Wigmore Street, Lawleys in Regent Street and Thomas Goode in South Audley Street are worth a visit; while for gold and silver the London Silver Vaults in Holborn are a must, as well as several individual shops in Bond Street and Kings Road.

Charing Cross Road is the centre of London's book trade with Foyle's at the north end pre-eminent. They'll usually have the book somewhere; the question is can it be found on their superbly stocked shelves? The British Museum has many specialist bookshops, too, and most of the big stores have excellent book departments, Harrods among them of course.

But it may well be that an entertaining day in one of London's many street markets will do just as well and save money into the bargain, which it usually is when bought in a market.

The rules of the game are that you get what you pay for; that you haggle with the stallholder until you are both satisfied with the price. If you are not, don't buy it. The markets are bustling places in which the stallholder needs to sell his stock out on the day, so he will be a fast-moving, fast-talking salesman, but honest, although he will not go out of his way to give you a bargain.

The most famous market is Petticoat Lane in London's East End, open on Sunday mornings when the crowds will be at their biggest and the entertainment at its peak. It sells just about everything, including animals, materials and curios.

Across the other side of London the Portobello Market is the centre of London's second hand antique trade. Saturday morning is the best time to go, but bargains are few and far between. Another antique market is in Camden Passage, Islington, where silver is the speciality.

Food markets are plentiful and the pick of them are Leather Lane in Holborn with fruit and vegetables taking pride of place among crockery and glassware, Berwick Street in Soho for the same combination and Billingsgate and Smithfield for fish and meat. Billingsgate has been going for about 300 years and, like Smithfield, is worth a visit if only for the atmosphere and characters.

So whatever your need, London will probably stock it.

Four of London's traffic wardens, pictured in an unfamiliar role, playing for the camera right. An unusually deserted Piccadilly Circus is shown overleaf by night.

High-kicking dancers and exotic – or minimal – costumes are all part of the entertainment scene. Top left, above and right: *Talk of the Town*. Left: *Raymonds Revue Bar*. Below: *La Valbonne*.

A magnificent night-time panorama, showing the Clock Tower of Big Ben, the Houses of Parliament and, beyond, the River Thames, is pictured overleaf.

78

81

London Pageantry

LONDON is rich in pageantry. At almost any time of the year it can be glimpsed by the discerning visitor, while to many Londoners it has become almost an unremarkable part of daily life, be it the Changing of the Guard in the forecourt of Buckingham Palace, the cheery Beefeater in his sumptuous uniform at the Tower, the Chelsea Pensioners occasionally to be seen taking the sun along the Chelsea Embankment, or even the old brewer's dray with its top-hatted driver perched high above the magnificent horse-drawn relic of Edwardian days. All these, in their different ways, are part of London's heritage.

But to most people the city's pageantry means the beautiful set-pieces brilliantly stage-managed every year in a style internationally acknowledged to be second to none; such events as the Lord Mayor's Show, the State Opening of Parliament and Trooping the Colour.

The Lord Mayor's Show: This is held on the first Saturday after the 9th November – the day on which, each year, a new Lord Mayor is elected. A long, colourful procession of carriages and floats, at times resembling more a carnival in atmosphere, winds its way through streets lined with cheering Londoners, from the Guildhall, the City's seat of government, to the Law Courts in the Strand. It is led by the new Mayor waving to his citizens from a beautiful coach built in 1757 and drawn by six magnificent brewers' horses. He has an escort of pikemen resplendent in the old uniforms of the Honourable Artillery Company of Pikemen and Musketeers, thought to be the oldest regiment in the world still in existence. His coach is followed by detachments from the three armed services accompanied by military bands. Each year the procession has a theme – flowers, the river, old London and so on – which is reflected in a series of beautifully designed floats put together by City associations, companies, guilds etc. The ceremony has its origins in the agreement made seven hundred years ago with King John which guaranteed the city's independence, in return for which each year the new Mayor should travel from the City to pay his respects to the Monarch. It certainly sets London alight on what is usually a damp, drizzly November day.

State Opening of Parliament: Each new session of Parliament, since the Commons has been sitting in Westminster, has been opened by a speech from the monarch of the day outlining the government's forthcoming legislative plans. The speech itself is usually remarkable for its lack of controversy or drama (it is written for the sovereign by the government of the time). But the procession to the House of Lords (the monarch always addresses her Lords with the Commons in attendance) from Buckingham Palace more than makes up for this. The Queen makes the journey in the superb Irish State Coach and is escorted by the Household Cavalry on their magnificent steeds. The short route is lined by the Brigade of Guards and the procession is, each year, Londoners' major opportunity to salute their Queen. The Opening is also marked by a 41-gun Royal Salute fired in nearby St James's Park.

Trooping the Colour: A "colour" is the ceremonial flag of a battalion or regiment, and "trooping" means marching to music. This splendid ceremony is held on the Sovereign's official birthday, the second Saturday in June (the Queen's actual birthday being 21 April). Dressed in the uniform of colonel of the regiment, she rides side-saddle from Buckingham Palace, down the Mall, turning right into Horseguards Parade just before Admiralty Arch. There she takes the salute as the scarlet-uniformed, bear-skinned Brigade of Guards (consisting of Grenadiers, Coldstreams, Scots, Irish and Welsh Guards), together with massed bands, put on an impressive display of precision marching. If it is a hot day it's not unusual for one or two guardsmen in their close-fitting uniforms to pass out on the parade ground, the event traditionally recorded in the following day's newspapers. But if it is wet, the ceremony is usually cancelled because of the damage the rain would do to the costly uniforms. Trooping the Colour is said to have evolved from the time in the British Army when, at the end of the day, no soldier could be dismissed from the parade ground until the colours of the regiment were safely lodged with the Commanding Officer. Then and only then, could a weary infantryman fall out and put his feet up after a heavy day's marching.

An altogether quieter act of pageantry, but no less moving, has been enacted at the Tower of London without fail every night for the past 700 years. This is the Ceremony of the Keys, in which the Tower's Chief Warder, in scarlet coat and medieval bonnet, locks the Tower and its valuable contents for the night. Admission is free but only a few people are allowed in to watch (many guide books explain how to ensure a visit).

At ten in the evening, the Tower virtually deserted, it has a moody, almost eerie atmosphere about it. One can imagine Sir Walter Raleigh pacing his cell or Anne Boleyn walking to her execution as the Warder, flickering lantern in one hand, the keys in the other, proceeds from gate to gate, turning the locks. As he approaches the Bloody Tower, a voice rings out:
"Halt. Who comes there?"
"The keys," he replies.
"Whose keys?"
"Queen Elizabeth's keys."
And after a dramatic pause, "Pass Queen Elizabeth's keys – and all's well." "God preserve Queen Elizabeth," shouts the Chief Warder; the stirring "Last Post" is sounded by a bugler and as the final note echoes away into the night the clock strikes ten, and the Tower is once more secure.

In mid-October a new legal term begins, marked by a special service at Westminster Abbey for judges, in their ermine and scarlet, and Queen's Counsels (barristers) in silk gowns. After the service they walk in stately file to the House of Lords where they have "breakfast" (actually a lunch) with the chief Law Lord, the Lord Chancellor.

These are but a few of the pageants of London which bring to those who watch them an indelible sense of the tradition and history inherent in the city.

There are many famous shopping areas in London and none more so than Burlington Arcade right. The Arcade was completed in 1819 and provides a traffic-free haven for shoppers, just off busy Piccadilly.

Large cities the world over have a wealth of
shopping facilities, and London has more than
most. In addition to the many individual
establishments, the boutiques and the specialist
shops catering for a wide variety of interests,
there are numerous large department stores
which, again, cater for all tastes and pockets,
from the everyday to highly priced and exotic.

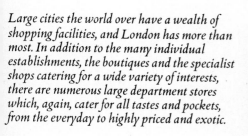

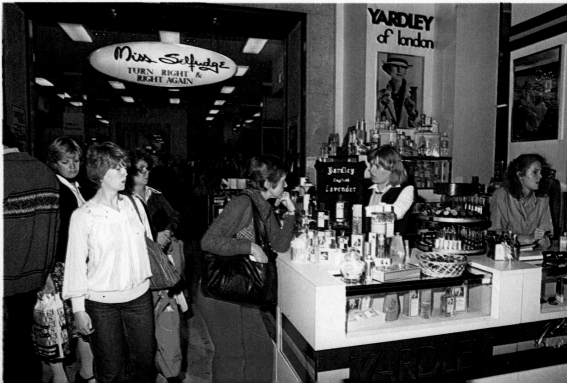

The crowned and blindfolded figure of Justice above stands atop the most famous of London's Courts; the Old Bailey.
Featured left are the impressive, and recently cleaned, Law Courts in Temple Bar.
The smoke and grime of the years has also been removed from the stonework of the City of London Guildhall below left.

Known simply as The Monument, the structure below was built in 1672-7 to commemorate the Great Fire of London which started in 1666 and raged for five days, leaving two thirds of London devastated.

The Lord Mayor of London's beautiful and elaborately decorated coach above right dates from 1757 and, when not in use, may be seen in the Guildhall Museum.

Pub lunches below right are very much a feature of mid-day London.

The view overleaf shows the Bank of England on the left and the beautiful façade of the Royal Exchange in the center.

Of London's many open spaces and parks, Hampstead Heath, top left has long been a firm favorite. Here there is space in which to walk (it occupies an area of almost 800 acres), fish top, bathe, ride and fly kites or simply sit and watch everyone else indulging their favorite pastimes. Above is the Golden Yard at Hampstead and bottom left the charming Georgian mansion, Kenwood House.

A Narrow Boat, left now used for pleasure cruises, makes its way towards Camden Lock, on the Regent's Park Canal.

Several famous people are buried in Highgate Cemetery, including Karl Marx, whose monument is shown below.

London's pubs range from the ultra-modern to the traditional. Pictured *above right is the Old Bull and Bush, and center right, the Horse and Groom, both in Hampstead. The Flask, bottom right is in Highgate.*

It is many years now since the Beatles pop group left their native Liverpool and achieved world-wide fame. Shown below is Abbey Road, immortalized by the group on one of their albums.

The aptly-named 'Little Venice' is a basin of the Grand Union Canal left. Some parts of London's old canal system have now been reclaimed, and pleasure barges now carry visitors along this intriguing waterway of the capital, skirting Regent's Park and providing a preview of some of the animals in the Zoo, which runs alongside the canal.

Regent's Park Zoo occupies an area on the north side of Regent's Park and it contains the most representative of the world's collections of animals. Some 5,000 animals are housed in this, one of the oldest zoos in the world; not only such favorites as elephants, polar bears, giraffes and leopards, but also more unusual species such as the Giant Panda, difficult to keep and even more difficult to breed in captivity.

The Garter Ceremony overleaf takes place at Windsor Castle, a very beautiful and historic location. This colorful ceremony always attracts large crowds.

Fittingly occupying the last page of a book on London is the lovely structure of St Paul's Cathedral page 96.

First published in Great Britain 1979 by Colour Library International Ltd.
© Illustrations: Colour Library International Ltd.
Colour separations by La Cromolito, Milan, Italy.
Display and text filmsetting by Focus Photoset, London, England.
Printed and bound by Rieusset, Barcelona, Spain.
I.S.B.N. 0-8317-5616-0 Library of Congress Catalogue Card N.º 79-2043
Published in the United States of America by Mayflower Books, Inc., New York City
Published in Canada by Wm. Collins and Sons, Toronto